Medjugorje

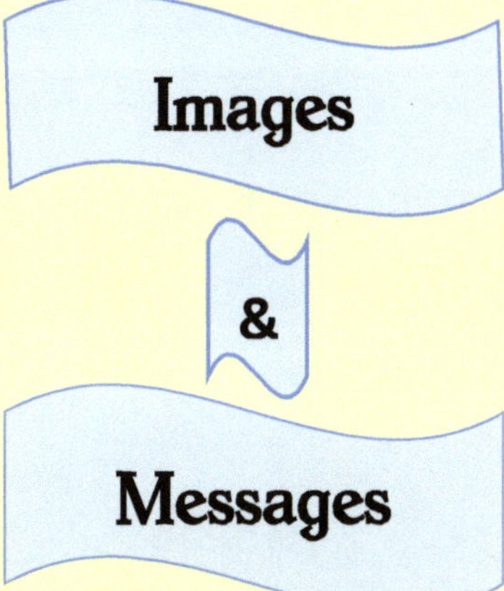

Images

&

Messages

Orsolya
Eden

Imprint:

*Orsolya Eden**
c/o AutorenServices.de
Birkenallee 24
36037 Fulda
Germany

* Please don´t send any parcels to this address.
If you would like to send a parcel to me, please enquire
first via e - mail for a separate address.
Thank you for your understanding.

E - mail: Orsolyaeden1@use.startmail.com

Cover design, illustration and photos: Orsolya Eden
Translation: Orsolya Eden
Note: Orsolya Eden is a pen name.
ISBN paperback: 978-3-949222-01-6

Glory be to the Father and the Son and the Holy Spirit and gratitude to the Blessed Virgin Mary

In thanksgiving to Felicitas, Richard and Cäcilia

Message from July 2, 2009 [1]

„Dear children! I am calling you because I need you. I need hearts ready for immeasurable love – hearts that are not burdened by vanity – hearts that are ready to love as my Son loved – that are ready to sacrifice themselves as my Son sacrificed himself. I need you. In order to come with me, forgive yourselves, forgive others and adore my Son. Adore him also for those who have not come to know him, those who do not love him. Therefore, I need you; therefore, I call you. Thank you."

---

[1] Giovani Luca Zenga (Translator*), Medjugorje 1981 - 2019 History of the apparitions and the messages of the Queen of Peace from 1981 to 2019*, Matica Hrvatska Čitluk, Čitluk - Medjugorje 2019, p. 193.

Message from September 12, 1985 [2]

"Dear children! I wish to tell you that the cross should be central these days. Pray especially before the cross from which great graces are coming. Now in your homes make a special consecration to the cross. Promise that you will neither offend Jesus nor abuse the cross. Thank you for having responded to my call."

[2] Giovani Luca Zenga (Translator), *Medjugorje 1981 - 2019 History of the apparitions and the messages of the Queen of Peace from 1981 to 2019*, Matica Hrvatska Čitluk, Čitluk - Medjugorje 2019, p. 28.

Message from August 25, 1997 [3]

"Dear children! God gives me this time as a gift to you, so that I may instruct and lead you on the path of salvation. Dear children, now you do not comprehend this grace, but soon a time will come when you will lament for these messages. But this is why, little children, live all of the words which I have given you through this time of grace and renew prayer, until prayer becomes a joy for you. Especially, I call all those who have consecrated themselves to my Immaculate Heart to become an example to others. I call all priests and religious brothers and sisters to pray the rosary and to teach others to pray. The rosary, little children, is especially dear to me. Through the rosary open your heart to me and I am able to help you. Thank you for having responded to my call."

[3] Giovani Luca Zenga (Translator), *Medjugorje 1981 - 2019 History of the apparitions and the messages of the Queen of Peace from 1981 to 2019*, Matica Hrvatska Čitluk, Čitluk - Medjugorje 2019, p. 91.

Message from January 2, 2019 [4]

"Dear children! Sadly among you, my children, there is so much battle, hatred, personal interests and selfishness. My children, so easily you forget my Son, His words, His love. Faith is being extinguished in many souls, and hearts are being grasped by material things of the world. But my motherly heart knows that there are still those who believe and love, and who are seeking how to draw all the closer to my Son, who are tirelessly seeking my Son – then in this way, they are also seeking me. These are the humble and the meek with their pain and suffering which they carry in silence with their hopes, and above all, with their faith. These are the apostles of my love, I am teaching you that my Son is not only asking for continuous prayers, but also for works and feelings – that you believe, that you pray, that with your personal prayers you grow in faith, that you grow in love. To love each other is what He asks for – that is the way to eternal life. My children, do not forget, that my Son brought the light to this world, and He brought it to those who wanted to see it and receive it. You be those, because this is the light of truth, peace and love. I am leading you in a

---

[4] Giovani Luca Zenga (Translator*), Medjugorje 1981 - 2019 History of the apparitions and the messages of the Queen of Peace from 1981 to 2019*, Matica Hrvatska Čitluk, Čitluk - Medjugorje 2019, p. 259.

motherly way to adore my Son; that you love my
Son with me; that your thoughts words and
actions may be directed to my Son – that they may
be in his name. Then my heart will be fulfilled.
Thank you. "

**Drops emanating from the knee of the
Statue of the Risen Christ**

Message from January 25, 1991[5]

"Dear children! Today like never before, I invite you to prayer. Let your prayer be a prayer for peace. Satan is strong and desires to destroy not only human life, but also nature and the planet on which you live. Therefore, dear children, pray that through prayer you can protect yourselves with God´s blessing of peace. God has sent me among you so that I may help you. If you so wish, grasp for the rosary. Even the rosary alone can work miracles in the world and in your lives. I bless you and remain with you for as long as it is God´s will. Thank you for not betraying my presence here and I thank you because your response is serving the good and the peace."

---

[5] Giovani Luca Zenga (Translator), *Medjugorje 1981 - 2019 History of the apparitions and the messages of the Queen of Peace from 1981 to 2019*, Matica Hrvatska Čitluk, Čitluk - Medjugorje 2019, p. 262.

Oval Sun

Message from February 2, 2019 [6]

Dear children! The love and goodness of the Heavenly Father give revelations which make faith grow, for it to be interpreted, that it may bring peace, certainty and hope. In this way, I, too, my children - through the merciful love of the Heavenly Father - always, anew, am showing you the way to my Son, to eternal salvation. But, unfortunately, many of my children do not want to hear me; many of my children are of two minds. And I - I always, in time and beyond time, magnified the Lord for all that He has done in me and through me. My Son gives Himself to you and breaks the bread with you. He speaks the words of eternal life to you so that you may carry them to everyone. And you, my children, apostles of my love, what are you afraid of when my Son is with you? Offer your souls to Him so that He can be in them and that He can make you instruments of faith, instruments of love. My children, live the Gospel, live merciful love for your neighbours, and, above all, life love for the Heavenly Father. My children, you are not united by chance. The Heavenly Father does not unite anyone by chance. My Son speaks to your souls. I speak to your heart.

---

[6] Giovani Luca Zenga (Translator*), Medjugorje 1981 - 2019 History of the apparitions and the messages of the Queen of Peace from 1981 to 2019*, Matica Hrvatska Čitluk, Čitluk - Medjugorje 2019, p. 259, 260.

As a mother I am saying to you: set out with me, love one another, give witness. Do not be afraid, with your example, to defend the truth - the Word of God which is eternal and never changes. My children, whoever acts in the light of merciful love and truth is always helped by Heaven and is not alone. Apostles of my love, may you always be recognized among all others by your hiddenness, love and radiance. I am with you. Thank you."

Message from March 2, 2018 [7]

Dear children, great are the works that the Heavenly Father has done in me, as He does in all those who love Him tenderly and who faithfully and devoutly serve Him. My children, the Heavenly Father loves you, and it is through His love that I am here with you. He is speaking to you. Why do you not desire to see the signs? Everything is easier alongside Him. Also pain lived with Him is easier because faith exists. Faith helps in the pain, and pain without faith leads to despair. Pain lived and offered to God raises up. Did my Son not redeem the world through His painful sacrifice? As His mother I was with Him in the pain and suffering, as I am with all of you. My children, I am with you in life, in suffering, in pain, in joy and in love.

Therefore, have hope. It is hope that makes you comprehend that life is there. My children, I am speaking to you, my voice is speaking to your soul, my heart is speaking to your heart. Oh, apostles of my love, how much my motherly heart loves you. How many things I desire to teach you. How my motherly heart desires that you be complete, and

---

[7] Giovani Luca Zenga (Translator*), Medjugorje 1981 - 2019 History of the apparitions and the messages of the Queen of Peace from 1981 to 2019*, Matica Hrvatska Čitluk, Čitluk - Medjugorje 2019, p. 250, 251.

you can be complete only when your soul, body and love are united within you. I implore you as my children, pray much for the Church and her servants – your shepherds; that the Church may be such as my Son desires – clear as spring water and full of love. Thank you."

Message from July 21, 1982 [8]

"There are many souls in Purgatory. There are also persons who have been consecrated to God: some priests, some religious. Pray for their intentions, at least seven Our Father´s, Hail Mary´s and Glory Be´s and the Creed. I recommend it to you. There is a large number of souls who have been in Purgatory for a long time because no one prays for them. A response to a question on fasting: The best fast is on bread and water. Through fasting and prayer, one can stop wars, one can suspend the laws of nature. Charity cannot replace fasting. (CP 69)"

---

[8] Medjugorje - Apologia.com, *The Messages of Medjugorje: The Complete Text, 1981 - 2014*, 2014, p. 49.

Message from July 25, 1982 [9]

"A response to questions which were asked concerning Hell: Today many persons go to Hell. God permits his children to suffer in Hell due to the fact that they have committed grave unpardonable sins. Those who are in Hell, no longer have a chance to know a better lot. (CP 71)

Response to questions regarding cures: for the cure of the sick, it is important to say the following prayers: the Creed, seven Our Father´s, Hail Mary´s and Glory Be´s and to fast on bread and water. It is good to impose one´s hands on the sick and pray. It is good to anoint the sick with holy oil. All priests do not have the gift of healing. In order to revive this gift, the priest must pray with perseverance and believe firmly. (CP 71)."

[9] Medjugorje - Apologia.com, *The Messages of Medjugorje: The Complete Text, 1981 - 2014*, 2014, p. 49.

INRI

Message from 1984 - 1985 [10]

"On the matter of a Catholic priest, confused because of the cure of an Orthodox child: Tell this priest, tell everyone, that it is you who is divided on earth. The Muslims and the Orthodox, for the same reason as Catholics, are equal before my Son and me. You are all my children. Certainly, all religions are not equal, but all men are equal before God, as St. Paul says. It does not suffice to belong to the Catholic Church to be saved, but it is necessary to respect the commandments of God in following one´s conscience. Those who are not Catholics, are no less creatures made in the image of God, and destined to rejoin someday, the House of the Father, Salvation is available to everyone, without exception. Only those who refuse God deliberately, are condemned. To him, who has been given little, little will be asked for. To whomever has been given much (to Catholics), very much will be required. It is God alone, in His infinite justice, Who determines the degree of responsibility and pronounces judgment. (C128)."

---

[10] Medjugorje - Apologia.com, *The Messages of Medjugorje: The Complete Text, 1981 - 2014*, 2014, p. 104.

IC XC
Ὁ ὪN
JESU TIBI CONFIDO

Message from October 2, 2011[11]

"Dear children; Also today my motherly heart calls you to prayer, to your personal relationship with God the Father, to the joy of prayer in Him. God the Father is not far away from you and He is not unknown to you. He revealed Himself to you through my Son and gave you Life that is my Son. Therefore, my children, do not give in to temptations that want to separate you from God the Father. Pray! Do not attempt to have families and societies without Him. Pray! Pray that your hearts may be flooded with the goodness that only comes from my Son. Who is sincere goodness. Only hearts filled with goodness can comprehend and accept God the Father. I will continue to lead you. In a special way I implore you not to judge your shepherds. My children, are you forgetting that God the Father called them? Pray! Thank you." Mirjana said: I have never said anything before, but you are aware brothers and sisters, that the Mother of God was with us? Each of us should ask himself: `Are you worthy of this?´ I am saying this because it is difficult for me to see her (Our Lady) in pain, because each of us is seeking a

---

[11] Giovani Luca Zenga (Translator), *Medjugorje 1981 - 2019 History of the apparitions and the messages of the Queen of Peace from 1981 to 2019*, Matica Hrvatska Čitluk, Čitluk - Medjugorje 2019, p. 203.

miracle, but does not want to work a miracle in himself.

Message from August 2, 2018 [12]

"Dear children, with a motherly love I am calling you to open your hearts to peace; to open your hearts to my Son, so that in your hearts love for my Son may sing, because only out of that love peace comes in the soul. My children, I know that you have goodness, I know that you have love - a merciful love, but many of my children still have a closed heart. They think that they can do it without directing their thoughts towards the Heavenly Father who illuminates - towards my Son who is always with you anew in the Eucharist and who desires to listen to you. My children why do you not speak to Him? The life of each of you is important and precious, because it is a gift from the Heavenly Father for eternity. Therefore, do not ever forget to keep on thanking Him: speak to Him. I know, my children, that what is to come afterwards is unknown to you, but when your hereafter comes you will receive all the answers. My motherly love desires that you be ready. My children, by your life keep putting good feelings in the hearts of people whom you meet, feelings of peace, goodness, love and forgiveness. Through

---

[12] Giovani Luca Zenga (Translator), *Medjugorje 1981 - 2019 History of the apparitions and the messages of the Queen of Peace from 1981 to 2019*, Matica Hrvatska Čitluk, Čitluk - Medjugorje 2019, p. 255.

prayer, hearken to what My Son is saying and act accordingly. Anew, I am calling you to prayer for your shepherds, for those whom my Son has called. Remember that they need prayers and love. Thank you."

Message from October 10, 1985 [13]

"Dear children! I wish also today to call you to live the messages in the parish. Especially I wish to call the youth of the parish, who are dear to me. Dear children, if you live the messages, you are living the seed of holiness. I, as the Mother, wish to call you all to holiness so that you can bestow it on others. You are a mirror to others! Thank you for having responded to my call."

---

[13] Giovani Luca Zenga (Translator*), Medjugorje 1981 - 2019 History of the apparitions and the messages of the Queen of Peace from 1981 to 2019*, Matica Hrvatska Čitluk, Čitluk - Medjugorje 2019, p. 29.

**Modified in form and levitating Križevac -
- Cross**

Message from November 2, 2019 [14]

"Dear children, my beloved Son always prayed and glorified the Heavenly Father. He always said everything to Him and trusted in His will. This is what you, my children, should also do, because the Heavenly Father always listens to His children. One heart in one heart – love, light and life.

The Heavenly Father gave Himself through a human face, and this face is the face of my Son. You, apostles of my love, you should always carry the face of my Son in your hearts and your thoughts. You should always think of His love and His sacrifice. You should pray to always feel His presence, because, apostles of my love, that is the way for you to help all those who do not know my Son, who have not come to know His love.

My children, read the book of the Gospel. It is always something new, it is what binds you to my Son who was born to bring the words of life to all of my children and to sacrifice Himself for all. Apostles of my love, carried by the love for my Son, bring love and peace to all of your brothers.

____

[14] Medjugorje Web Site, „*Our Lady of Medjugorje Messages of year 2019*" in www.medjugorje.ws under: https://www.medjugorje.ws/en/messages/2019/ (retrieved on 30 July 2020).

Judge no one. Love everyone according to the love for my Son. In this way, you will also be caring for your soul, and it [your soul] is that which is most precious, which truly belongs to you. Thank you. ”

Message from May 25, 2010 [15]

"Dear children! God gave you the grace to live and to defend all the good that is in you and around you, and to inspire others to be better and holier; but Satan, too, does not sleep and through modernism diverts you and leads you to his way. Therefore, little children, in the love for my Immaculate Heart, love God above everything and live His commandments. In this way, your life will have meaning and peace will rule on earth. Thank you for having responded to my call."

[15] Medjugorje - Apologia.com, *The Messages of Medjugorje: The Complete Text, 1981 - 2014*, 2014, p. 138.

At the end of the shopping street, a possible ascent to Apparition Hill.

Message from October 25, 1993 [16]

"Dear children! These years I have been calling you to pray, to live what I am telling you, but you are living my messages a little. You talk, but do not live, that is why little children, this war is lasting so long. I invite you to open yourselves to God and in your hearts to live with God, living the good and giving witness to my messages. I love you and wish to protect you from every evil, but you do not desire it. Dear children, I cannot help you if you do not live God's commandments, if you do not live the mass, if you do not give up sin. I invite you to be apostles of love and goodness. In this world of unrest give witness to God and God's love, and God will bless you and give you what you seek from Him. Thank you for having responded to my call. "

---

[16] Medjugorje - Apologia.com, *The Messages of Medjugorje: The Complete Text, 1981 - 2014*, 2014, p. 49.

The Child Jesus in the arms of His Mother Mary

www.ingramcontent.com/pod-product-compliance
Lightning Source LLC
LaVergne TN
LVHW051456180726
843512LV00001B/62